THE LAST DAYS OF STEAM

Robert and Bruce
Wheatley

The
Last Days
of Steam
on Australia's Railways

Angus and Robertson

First published in 1971 by
ANGUS & ROBERTSON LTD
221 George Street, Sydney
107 Elizabeth Street, Melbourne
89 Anson Road, Singapore
54 Bartholomew Close, London

National Library of
Australia card number and
ISBN 0 207 12134 6

PRINTED IN HONG KONG

STEAM ON THE RAIL SCENE

From early childhood we had shown a keen interest in steam engines. Some nights near our home we would hear the rhythmic beat of the exhaust as the engines struggled up the grade — often slipping on the wet rails. By day we watched in fascination as the expresses roared through our town, the distinctive blast of their whistles heralding their progress. This kindled a real desire to see steam engines in action farther afield. So it was, my brother barely a teenager, and I only a few years older, set off to broaden our interest and fulfil a sense of adventure.

When we think of the years we roamed over the State of New South Wales, on all types of trains, the sleepless nights, the slow and monotonous hours travelling on goods trains, the freezing times spent photographing steam at night, the hospitality of railway staff, the friendly talks as we shared a welcome cup of tea — there arises a flood of memories that will grow stronger as the years roll by.

Steam engines have a strong appeal, an atmosphere of their own, almost as alive as the men who work them. For the crew, to drive a steam engine is a harsh and tedious job, exposed to all weathers. But for every bit of harshness there is a something just short of beauty. To see the animated power of a steam engine at work, or a trail of steam in the cold morning air, or at night the plumes of raging gold on the steam and smoke as the fireman struggles to feed the monster's heart, or the engine lose traction and go into a frenzied skid, the driver quickly acting to restore adhesion to the massive driving wheels — is to see man and machine unite in perfect working harmony, in a display of grandeur unparalleled by any other machine that man has invented.

The sense of adventure, of the unexpected, the challenge to capture on film the true impact of steam, has provided us with a most rewarding hobby and a lasting sense of satisfaction. . . . Perhaps you can share it here.

THE PHOTOGRAPHS

1. Class leader 3801, resplendent in its green livery, rounds a bend near Bundanoon, in charge of the last steam-hauled Southern Highlands Express. This train marked the end of steam working on the main southern line. 11th October, 1969.

2. In the last few weeks of mainline steam operation out of Sydney-Central, 3813 stands at No. 5 platform prior to its departure for the southern highlands town of Moss Vale on 25th September, 1969.

3. Assigned to banking duties, 5390 is turned at Murrurundi loco on 17th May, 1965 in preparation for the next train requiring assistance (3526 next page) over the steeply graded Liverpool Ranges. But for Murrurundi loco, time was running out, as a crippling drought brought an acute water shortage, resulting in what was to be its permanent closure in June 1965. Steam banking duties were then taken over by diesel electric units based at Werris Creek.

4. Leaving Murrurundi township and the loco depot behind, 3526 heads its load northwards to tackle the 1 in 40 grade over the Liverpool Range with 5390 pushing at the rear on 17th May, 1965.

Numbering 35 in all, the C-35 class entered service from 1914, and were yet another passenger loco to see extensive service on goods working in the latter days of northern steam.

5. In the cool of a misty spring morning in 1968, 3638 lifts its load through the typically English countryside at Burradoo, 84 miles south of Sydney.

6. Trailing steam hangs heavy in the air while a morning mist clears over the hills near Burrawang, as 3077 dashes toward Robertson in its last week of steam operation on the cross-country link between Moss Vale and Wollongong. 11th February, 1967.

7. Three miles of reverse 12-chain radius curves on a nearly continuous 1 in 40 grade form the Tumulla Bank over the Stringy Bark Range. Most passenger and goods trains needed assistance over this range, 158 miles west from Sydney.

At George's Plains (at the foot of the range) bank engines were attached, either marshalled in the lead or pushing uncoupled at the rear, to assist trains to reach the summit.

Approaching the crossing loop at Tumulla, bank engine 5412 gives assistance to 3609 as they battle up the grade, on 8th September, 1965.

8. On the Moonbi Ranges, situated between Tamworth and Armidale, 3531 climbs the 1 in 40 grade with a load of superphosphate bound for Walcha Road. 18th May, 1965.

9. On a rainy night in January, 1967, the murky depth of Broadmeadow loco reveals 5907, 3532, 5913, 3646, and a 53 class. 5907 and 3532 had both come in from duties from Gosford, while 3646 prepares to work the Glen Innes Mail to Werris Creek.

10. 3662 and 3630 simmer in Bathurst running sheds on a freezing night in July, 1966, as 3013 takes a spell from shunting duties.

11. Wallerawang station comes alive with the hiss of escaping steam, as the rhythmic pump of the air-compressor echoes through the yards. The driver of 3649 waits patiently as the parcels are transferred from the brake van, before he ushers his charge into the night. 11th January, 1967.

12. Of the thirty 38 class built, only the first five received streamlining (3801 to 3805). Never did the streamlined 38s look more in place than on air-conditioned expresses. Here 3803 is seen speeding through Narara on the Newcastle Flyer on 24th May, 1965.

13. In true western style, 6018 receives assistance from 5369 up Tumulla Bank. At this stage, the western Garratts were being used 22 out of 24 hours a day, in order to cope with the huge volume of traffic. 5th September, 1964.

14. On a winter's evening in 1966, light rain falls at Gosford, as another Garratt locomotive prepares to depart. With electrification completed as far as Gosford by 1960, a change of motive power was necessitated for the haul farther north.

With the crew successfully transferred to the Garratt, 6016 prepares to lift its tonnage northwards to Broadmeadow.

15. Following its steady climb from Picton, 3654 waits for the road at Moss Vale, after watering and shovelling down.

16. The crisp autumn air is filled by the clipped staccato exhaust of 3828 as it hurriedly shifts the Southern Highlands Express out of Moss Vale. 19th May, 1967.

17. On the last leg of its long run from the border, 3612 takes charge of the Brisbane Express (via Wallangarra) accelerating through Broadmeadow yards on 29th September, 1967.

A unique arrangement using 3 different types of motive power operated for some time on this express. It was electrically hauled for the first 50 miles from Sydney (Central) to Gosford; then by steam for the next 205 miles to Werris Creek, and then by diesel electric for the final 237 miles through to the Queensland border.

18, 19. 5903 and 3249 undergo repairs at Enfield loco. April, 1968.

20. From November, 1968 through to May, 1969, steam made a surprise comeback on the North Coast line. With the dieselization of the Maitland-Taree section completed in August, 1958, it remained dieselized until an acute locomotive shortage saw the reintroduction of steam working.

Here, late in the afternoon of 24th May, 1969, on the last of these workings to Taree, 5917 is crossed by 6017 on an "up" (i.e. a train heading towards Sydney) Newdell coal train at Maitland.

21. The 1.10 a.m. mixed from Central station seemed to have forgotten that time had moved on, almost oblivious to the rapid changes that were taking place around it. Always taking over 7 hours to do the 138 miles to Goulburn, it was the last mixed train to be hauled by steam.

With the sun low on the horizon, 3808 leaves Bundanoon, heading south, on 1st July, 1967.

22. 3642 Cowra loco, 19th November, 1966.

23. 3807 Orange loco, 24th March, 1967.

24.   On a rainy night two days before Christmas in 1966, parcels are unloaded in the twilight at Moss Vale station, after 3097 has completed its journey from Wollongong.

25.   With the electrification of large parts of the suburban system, many of the C-30 class had their side tanks, bunkers and rear bogies removed, and their frame shortened. Seventy-seven of the class which underwent this conversion were then known as the C-30T class, and spent much of their time on the country branch lines of the state.

3016, one of the locos to undergo conversion, departs Cowra on the Eugowra Mixed. 19th November, 1966.

26.   Running several hours late (through a derailment of a goods train earlier that night), the driver of 3659 gently eases out the regulator, in the pre-dawn light at Newbridge, heading the Coonamble Mail towards Blayney. 7th September, 1965.

27.   In the first light of dawn, 3803 heads the "up" Glen Innes Mail. 14th August, 1965.

28.   Enfield loco at dawn. 3001T, 3809, 5468. 27th April, 1968.

29.   Dim lighting casts its glow on 3224, 3282, 5901, 5235, 3246, 5429, and 3320, at No.1 roundhouse Enfield. 12th January, 1968.

30.   A short burst of sunlight between the clouds shines on 3668 as it uncouples from the train it has hauled from Lithgow. Bathurst, 16th July, 1966.

31.   3822 coasts No.28 Central West Express into George's Plains after its descent of Tumulla Bank. 8th September, 1965.

32.   With the movement of the massive 1968 wheat harvest barely underway, strong demands were placed on motive power, resulting in an acute locomotive shortage. By the end of November, 1968 thousands of tons of goods traffic had built up on the north coast line at Taree. With no end in sight to move the huge backlog, the decision was made to return steam to Taree, by utilizing Broadmeadow's 59 class, which were released from goods and local trip working in the week-ends.

Here, 5901 and 5917 on No. 525 "up" goods thunder out of Bundook, with the scenic backdrop of the lush North Coast dairy country. 4th May, 1969.

33.   As livestock graze near the railway line, 3088 approaches with caution as it heads the "down" Merriwa goods. 15th March, 1969.

34.   The 36 class, once the principal passenger engine, were affectionately known as ''Pigs'' (called such in the mid-1920s because of teething troubles, but later this was kept up because of the humped round boiler and firebox); they worked in large numbers on the west in the last years of steam. As dieselization allowed the reduction in the number of steam locos, many older goods engines were replaced by the newer and faster passenger engines. On a typical west working, ''Pig'' 30 works an ''up'' goods through Newbridge on 7th September, 1965.

35.   Ranking with the largest engines built in Europe, the 60 class 4-8-4 + 4-8-4 Beyer-Garratts were the most powerful steam locomotives in Australia. Their light axle load permitted their use on many sections of track which were restricted to other classes of locomotives.

Working an ''up'' Newdell coal train at Nundah, 6039 heads towards the coast. September, 1968.

36.   3813 on No. 50 Moss Vale passenger, crosses 3807 on the 1.10 a.m. mixed at Burradoo.

37.   On a Gosford passenger, 3827 works through thick fog at Kotara. 12th May, 1967.

38.   First introduced in 1891, the P class (as they were classified prior to 1924) were a very successful and popular engine. They were equally at home on goods or passenger trains in any part of the State. They were so popular, that even by the middle of the 1950s all were still in service.

At Armidale in May, 1965, 3315 accelerates through the outskirts of the city, northward bound on the Glen Innes Mail.

39.   Using steam shunters at depots provided many opportunities for steam to work through sections where diesel electrics held full sway.

Stifling 100-degree heat of a summer's day on 19th November, 1968, sees 5311 on transfer as yard shunter, departing Wingen on 243 goods bound for Werris Creek.

40.   The section of line between Gosford and Broadmeadow became the mecca for countless numbers of photographers, recording the many and varied motive power combinations this section of line had to offer — from tank engines on local passenger workings through to double headed Garratts on block loads.

A friendly chat precedes the departure of 3524 + 5456 on a ''down'' goods at Gosford on the 14th May, 1966.

41. 3326 and 3827 look impressive, but the air is impatient as the noise of screaming steam fills the cold night at Blayney, while the driver of 3326 waits for the road to be given for No. 49 Coonamble mail to proceed on its journey west. November, 1966.

42. The driver of 3236, on a cross-country goods between Binnaway and Dubbo. November, 1965.

43. Single line working over much of N.S.W. necessitated a foolproof system to ensure one train per section at any one time. At Dombarton signal box, the driver of 3093 exchanges staffs, giving him the right of way to take his two-car passenger train over the 1 in 30s, on the cross-country link to Moss Vale. 10th July, 1965.

44. By November, 1967, all 36 class had been withdrawn from service, because of a union ban on their inadequate reversing equipment for shunting trips. However, increasing traffic and a lack of diesels to replace steam power, led in 1968 to 6 of the class re-entering service with power reverse equipment, as well as many others in original condition.

Here "Pig" 38, first to be fitted with the power reverse equipment, rounds the bend into Mittagong on No. 335 goods in April, 1969.

45. In the afternoon sun, 3529 works through Broadmeadow yards on a relief passenger to Singleton. 12th May, 1967.

46. The crew of 3807 on No. 34 mixed wait for 3638 on a relief Easter passenger to clear the yards, before heading eastward from Orange. 24th March, 1967.

47. The shifting of the numerous bulk wheat trains from the wheat belt to the coast, regularly brought the system to saturation point for many months of the year.

After 6011 has brought its bulk wheat train into Molong from Dubbo, it receives assistance from 3644 as it heads towards Orange. 5th January, 1967.

48. 6015 works its way through the city of Orange on No. 65 goods bound for Dubbo on 4th March, 1967.

49. Sheep-skins are hurriedly loaded on to the Merriwa goods at Sandy Hollow, as an approaching rainstorm looms in the distance. 15th March, 1969.

50. Standing at Munna, a few miles north of Mudgee, 3306 (i.e. the 106th engine of the 32 class) works its way towards Binnaway. 23rd May, 1967.

51. In the early months of 1966, 36 class working on the west was still an everyday sight. With 4 miles of 1 in 70 ahead, 3647 lifts its load out of Blayney bound for Bathurst, on the 15th January, 1966.

52. With the allotting of diesel electric units to Bathurst depot, commencing in October, 1965, the 60 class Garratts working on the Lithgow-Orange section were the first steam to be displaced by the new form of motive power. However, 5 "light type" Garratts remained (i.e. those Garratts with 16 tons axle load) to work the Orange-Dubbo section, via Wellington and Molong.

After repairs at Bathurst loco, 6014 (a light type) works through Perthville on its way to Orange, through a section that at this time rarely vibrated to the steady 4 cylinder pound of the 60 class locomotive. August, 1966.

53. On an autumn morning, 3828 accelerates out of Moss Vale with the Southern Highlands Express. 19th May, 1967.

54. Steam was used extensively on the Richmond line during peak hours, to supplement the regular rail motors and diesel trains.

In the morning peak hour, 3322 gallops along between Riverstone and Schofields with a commuter train from Richmond. September, 1966.

55. On the Newcastle expresses the 38 class were never more at home. Even now the remaining 38 class still haul this express, a tribute to a class of engine on the highest pinnacle of steam passenger development in N.S.W.

Here 3820 races the morning Newcastle Express through Cardiff. 1st September, 1967.

56. An early morning scene down south, as 3828 departs Bowral on the Sydney-bound Moss Vale passenger. 11th February, 1967.

57. Leaving the city behind, 3810 heads towards Goulburn. 29th March, 1969.

58. Right on time, the crew of 3237 wait to leave Waratah on a Maitland passenger. December, 1968.

59. Guard, Merriwa goods.

60. In the heat of the late afternoon sun, 3606 and 3646 stand at Dubbo in charge of the Coonamble mail, at a time when all workings from this depot were steam-hauled. 16th January, 1964.

61. The railway town of Werris Creek (known by railway men as "The Creek") was the hub of railway operations for the north-west of the State.

On the 18th January, 1964, 5473 and 5912 pass through Werris Creek station, bound for Armidale.

62. Fresh out of overhaul, 3808 stands at Moss Vale station. 19th May, 1967.

63. Fireman at work. 3801.

64. 3808, 5408, 5325 and 5158 stand at the inspection pit at Enfield loco in the early hours of the morning. 27th April, 1968.

65. The winter sun pierces Port Waratah loco as 5139 prepares to commence duties for the day. Port Waratah loco was the last all-steam depot, supplying motive power for the never-ending flow of coal traffic in the Newcastle region. 30th August, 1968.

66. 3088 hurries towards Denman on the Merriwa goods. 27th April, 1968.

67. The allocation of 38 class Pacifics to goods working in the 1960s, kept many of the class from redundancy, as the new diesel electrics displaced them from long distance passenger haulage.

In late 1965, 3812 hurtles its load through Campbelltown, on a typical south steam working.

68. At Dunedoo, the steam gently rises into the still night air, as the crews exchange engines. The soft whine from the generators will soon give way to the muffled beat of 3233, as the driver eases his new charge towards Mudgee, only to be followed later by 3306 bound for Binnaway. 23rd May, 1967.

69. At Blayney, the escaping steam is blown by the cold night wind, in January, 1967. The driver had just transferred the carriages bound for Cowra into the opposite platform, allowing No. 49 Forbes mail to make its way farther west. After the clipped beat of 3810 dies in the distance, the only form of life left is in the yards, where a simmering standard goods engine awaits its turn to take its part of the mail to Cowra.

70. Towering billows of black smoke rise high over Central station, as 3809 prepares to depart No. 1 platform with the Southern Highlands Express on 21st March, 1969.

71.   3825 arrives at Moss Vale on 1st March, 1969 at the head of the "up" Southern Highlands Express. Soon the fireman would fill the 38s tender with water for the final 88 miles to Sydney.

72.   Depots for the servicing of steam locomotives were situated in almost every major town throughout the State, providing facilities for coaling, watering and turning of engines, as well as for running repairs.

At Cowra loco, engines are steamed up prior to their departure. 19th November, 1966.

73.   As well as the usual roundhouse, sheds were installed at many depots, one such depot being Bathurst, shown here on a winter's afternoon in July, 1966. "Pig" 65 had just been out-shopped from a "tone-up", while "Pig" 62 had been allotted to the Raglan Bank (the grade out of Bathurst to the east) as "push-up" engine while "Pig" 68 was to double head later in the night with 5429 to Cowra.

74.   3315 in spotless condition, stands at Armidale loco in preparation for the Glen Innes Mail. 19th May, 1965.

75.   Working round the clock, the coal drags from Newdell to Port Waratah provided constant employment for the Broadmeadow-based Garratts. Working out their last years, 6023 on a 1500-ton load passes 6027 returning with a load of empty wagons between Newdell and Singleton in October, 1969.

76.   The beautiful Liverpool Ranges provided a formidable barrier to trains in both directions. Most passenger and goods trains required assistance over the 1 in 40 grades on either side of the range, culminating in a tunnel near Ardglen station.

With the help of the banker engine 5390, attached at Willow Tree, 3675 is showered by its own cinders, as they struggle with a full load of wheat from the north west, bound for the coast, in 1965.

77.   "Shovelling down" operations were familiar at strategic points around the State, men being employed to shift the coal from the back of the tender to within easy reach of the fireman. One such place was Moss Vale, where 3638 is prepared for the final haul to the top of the highlands, as it double heads with 5902 on 10th May, 1969.

78.   A standard goods is de-ashed at Enfield, as the sun rises, 18th April, 1969.

79.   A friendly greeting by the fireman of "Pig" 18 as an "up" wheat train from Parkes passes at the crossing loop at Gamboola, west of Orange. 3618 was proceeding light engine to Molong, to assist another 36 class over the arduous 1 in 40 grades on the 23-mile section through to Orange East Fork Junction. 5th March, 1967.

80.   In the afternoon light at Euchareena, 26 miles north of Orange, 6040 is waylaid by 5343 + 6014 bound for Dubbo.

6040 was the last steam engine to enter service on the N.S.W. railways, in January 1957, and is now preserved as a static exhibit at Enfield Museum.

81.   In mid-1965, before the transfer of diesel electric units to Bathurst, the various depots on the main western line had allotted to them no less than 38 of the 36 class. These versatile engines at various times performed all duties, from working the Central West Express right down to banking duties.

At George's Plains 3624 assists 3636 as they prepare to tackle Tumulla Bank on the 8th September, 1965.

82.   5333 takes water at Blayney, on No. 41 Cowra goods. 8th January, 1966.

83.   The rising sun silhouettes billowing steam from 3617 as it lifts its load into Mittagong, in the middle of the 1967 winter.

84.   Heading into the night, 6029 ascends Whittingham Bank. 1st September, 1968.

14》
15》》

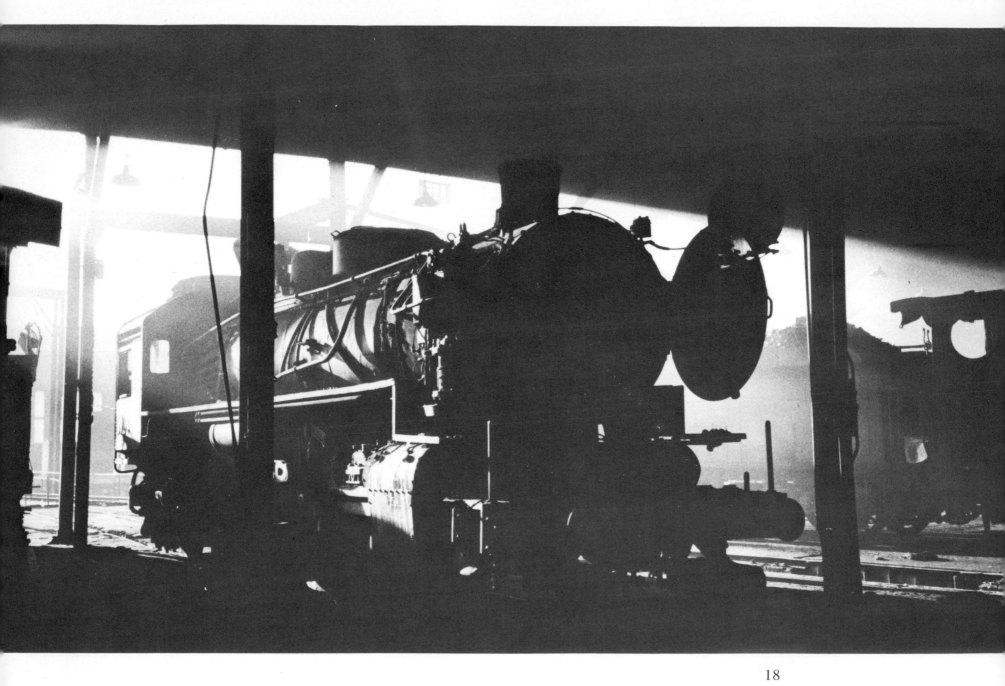

22

23

25
26》
27》》

28

29

30

31

35》

43》

44

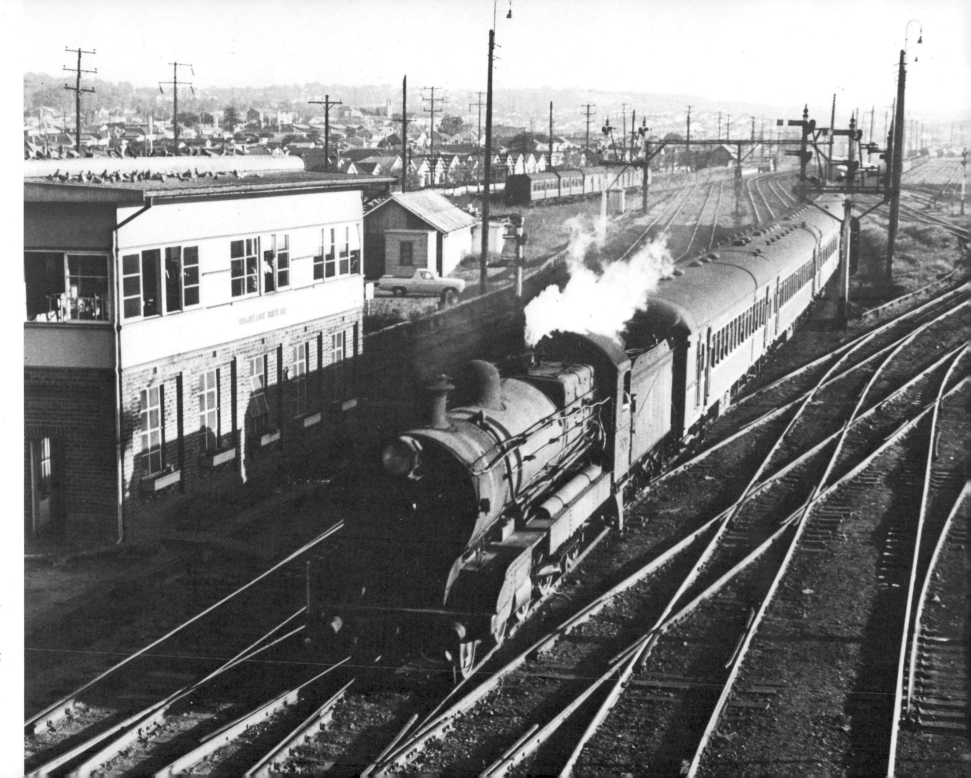

53

58

59

62》

63》》

61

72

73

81   82

83

84》